Enchanting Crafts

Over 30 ... your home

D&C
David and Charles
www.mycraftivity.com

* Editor:
  Catherine Dandres Franck
* Assistant editor:
  Helene Pouchot
* Illustrations:
  Pascale Etchecopar
* Photographs:
  Xavier Scheinkmann
* Production and layout
  Atelier Juliane Cordes

A DAVID & CHARLES BOOK
© Edilarge SA 2007
Editions Ouest-France, Rennes (35)
www.editionsouestfrance.fr
Originally published in France as *Un univers féerique*

First published in the UK in 2008 by
David & Charles
David & Charles is an F+W Publications
Inc. company
4700 East Galbraith Road
Cincinnati, OH 45236

ISBN-13: 978-0-7153-3004-3 paperback
ISBN-10: 0-7153-3004-7 paperback

Printed in France
for David & Charles
Brunel House   Newton Abbot   Devon

Visit our website at www.davidandcharles.co.uk

David & Charles books are available from all good
bookshops; alternatively you can contact our
Orderline on 0870 9908222 or write to us at
FREEPOST EX2 110, D&C Direct, Newton Abbot,
TQ12 4ZZ (no stamp required UK only);
US customers call 800-289-0963 and Canadian
customers call 800-840-5220.

Acknowledgments

'Thank you to *my family and my Prince
Charming,* who have helped me change
my pumpkin into a carriage.
And to *Justine, Léa, Juliette and Kerenn,*
mischievous little fairies who have
allowed themselves to be tamed.
I thank *Caroline* for the perfect timing
of her magic formulas. I also send a
thank you to the *town of Saumur* for the
support that it gives to young
creators. And finally, thanks to
Catherine for her trust.'

Contents

....*..*..*.*...*..*..*.*

A little magic lies within every one of us and all we
need to unlock it is a key.
Close your eyes and dream of a beautiful ethereal realm,
imagine discovering beautiful accesories, pampering beauty
treatments and delicious delights. Now open your eyes and find all
the secrets of this enchanted land right in front of you.
Live your fantasy and be inspired to go ahead and have fun
creating your own world filled with magic and sparkle.

Enchanted workshop

TOOLS

- Scissors

- Pins

- Flat-nosed pliers

- Cutting pliers

- Glue gun

- Iron

- Sewing machine, if possible

- Crochet hook (size 4)

- Knitting needles (size 10)

- Sewing needles

- Safety pin

DIFFERENT STITCHES USED

- Running stitch

- Backstitch

- Overcast stitch

- Blanket stitch

HOW TO MAKE A GATHERING THREAD

- **By hand:** sew a line of 5mm (¼in) running stitches line along the whole length of the fabric. When you reach the end, knot the thread on one side and push the fabric from the other end to gather it to the desired length.

- **By machine:** set to the widest possible running stitch. Sew a row of stitches along the fabric. Finish off the threads on one side, then gently pull the underneath thread at the other end. Pull up and gather the fabric until the desired length is reached.

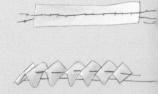

- The gathers can be made in fabric or ribbon, in the middle or at the edge of the material, depending on the desired result.

...Thread and beads
* nylon thread
* 11 large, transparent drop beads
* 10 small drop beads
* 10 small, opaque drop beads

...Accessories and tools
* scissors
* pretty brass clasp
* 2 knot covers 3mm (⅛in) in diameter, to match the clasp
* Flat-nosed pliers
* glue gun

Raindrop necklace

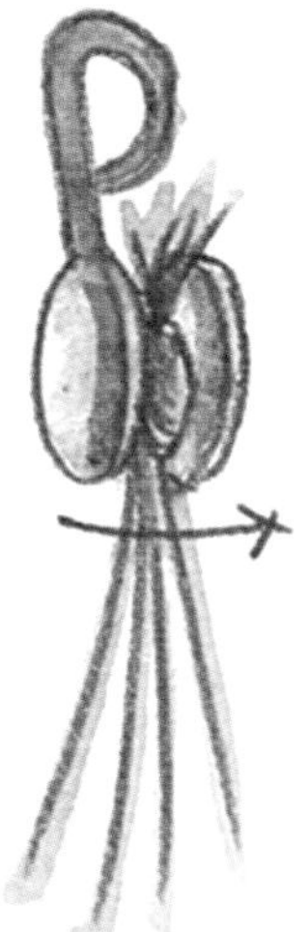

1 * Preparing the necklace
* Cut four nylon threads to the following lengths: 44cm (17in), 46cm (18in), 48cm (18¾in) and 50cm (20in). Tie the threads together at one end in a knot and conceal within a knot cover. Shut the cover tightly with flat-nosed pliers.

2 * Threading on the drop beads
* Lay the threads flat, with the shortest at the top, and the longest at the bottom. Thread on the beads as shown in the diagram. Gather the threads together and close the necklace using the other knot cover, then attach the clasp to each side.
* Space the beads so that they are attractively arranged; leave 10cm (4in) free before the knot covers. Using the glue gun, dot little drops of glue on to the threads on each side of the beads to prevent them from moving. Leave to dry for a few minutes.

10cm (4in)　　　　　　　　　10cm (4in)

Golden loop necklace

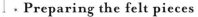

1 * Preparing the felt pieces

· Using the templates (see page 17), cut out
three flowers from white felt. Cut some
little strips 3mm (⅛in) wide and 4-10mm
(¼-½in) long from orange felt. Take
approximately 1m (1yd 4in) of orange
sewing thread, fold it in half and use to
embroider the irregular veins at the base
of the petals. Stitch the orange strips to
the centre like pistils and attach some gold
rocaille beads.

· Cut out five leaves in each shade of green
felt, varying the sizes. Put two strands
of sewing thread together in different
colours (either white and dark green
or white and orange) and randomly
embroider the veins.

2 * Finishing the flowers

· Sew two leaves on to the reverse of
each flower (six leaves in total).

3 * Distributing the crimping beads

· Thread seven large crimping beads on to
50cm (20in) of twisted wire without
closing them; fix the clasp with two othe
smaller beads; crimp straight away.

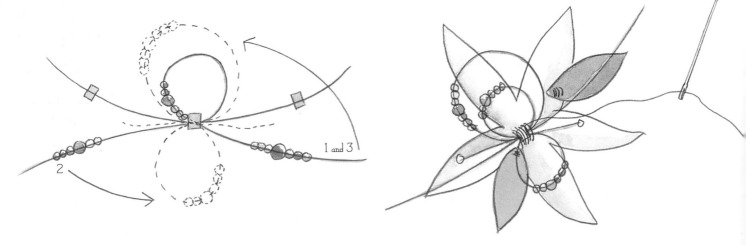

4 ⋆ Forming the loops

- Cut three twisted wires of 30cm (12in) in length, two of 21cm (8¼in) and two of 12.5cm (5in). Lay the necklace flat and place the centre crimping bead in the middle of the wire, then thread the 30cm (12in) wire through it. Thread some rocaille beads and a large bead on to each end of the wire.
- Thread each end of the wire through the crimping bead again, one end towards the top (1) and the other towards the bottom (2), to form a figure of eight. Then, add some beads to one side of the wire and thread it back through the crimping bead to make a second loop above (3).
- Adjust the loops by pulling them so that they look even, then fix them in place by tightening the crimping bead with the flat-nosed pliers.

- Repeat with the other two 30cm (12in) wires. Continue with the 12.5cm (5in) wires, making just one loop, then finish with two loops from the 21cm (8¼in) wires. Don't forget each time to thread some beads on to each loop.
- Using the glue gun, drop a blob of glue on to each end of the wire.

5 ⋆ Fixing the leaves

- At the centre of the necklace, attach the large flower to the crimping bead with sewing thread, then the two little flowers to the single loops at the sides. Fix a leaf to each of the remaining crimping beads with a drop of glue (see photo page 15).

Golden loop necklace, page 14 (actual size)

Cut out 3 times

Cut out 3 times

Cut out 4 times

Floral crown, page 18 (scale 60 per cent)

1

2   3

4

5   6   7   8

1 - netting in green
2 - netting in white
3 - netting in green
4 - netting in gold
5 - pink chiné felt
6 - pink chiné felt
7 - white felt
8 - white felt

* felt in pink chine and white
* netting in iridescent green, gold, light green and white
* 1.2m (1yd 11in) gold tiger tail
* sewing thread in white

...Beads and crystals...
* around 20 iridescent white rocaille beads
* 3 transparent rocaille beads
* 5 iridescent green rocaille beads
* 12 gold rocaille beads
* 4 opaque violet flower sequins
* 7 transparent violet flower sequins
* 12 iridescent violet crystals

* 7 silver metallic crystals
* 6 little flower sequins in shades of white and pink

...Accessories and tools...
* scissors
* needle

Floral crown

1 . Cut out the flowers

· Using the templates (see page 17), cut the flowers out of the felt and netting, then overlay them as in the diagram below. Using sewing thread, sew a cluster of rocaille beads into the centre of each one to secure the two layers.

2 . Attach the first flowers

· Slip the end of the tiger tail under the stitching on the back of the white netting flower, on the right in the photo. Make two stems 3cm (1¼in) long, at the bottom of which you should place a transparent violet flower sequin topped with an iridescent white rocaille bead. Pass the thread back through the sequin and knot it behind before returning it to the base by twisting it around the stem. Form a third, smaller stem decorated with an iridescent violet crystal.

3cm (1⅛in)

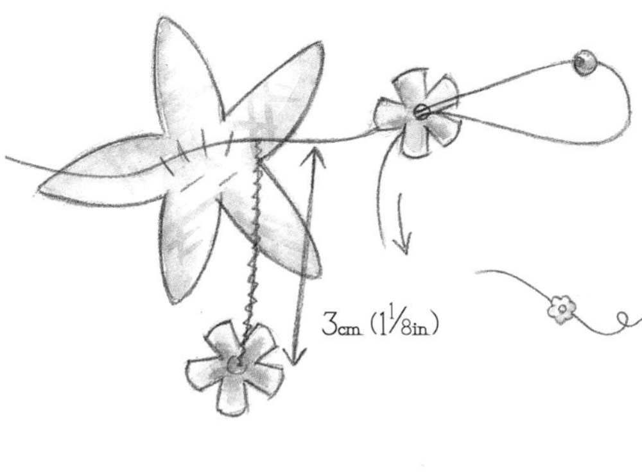

3 . Finishing the flowers

· Next, attach the large green flower: gently make a hole in the centre so that you can insert three 2.5cm (1in) pistils. Insert three opaque flower sequins each topped with a transparent rocaille bead.

· Attach the pink felt flower without adding the pistil, then the little white one. On the latter, create four 1cm (½i pistils coming from the centre and decorate each one with a silver metallic crystal. Add two pistils with transparent flower sequins topped with iridescent white rocaille beads and two others with an iridescent violet crystal, all coming from the back of this flower.

· Place the unused beads and sequins on the remaining thread, making little loo and stems until the size fits your head. Close the crown by tying a knot.

...Thread and beads...
* very fine gold tiger tail
* around 40 iridescent, transparent rocaille beads
* around 50 iridescent white mini rocaille beads

...Accessories and tools...
* cutting pliers
* pair of gold-coloured earring fastenings

Floral earrings

5mm (¹⁄₄in)

2cm (³⁄₄in)

5mm (¹⁄₄in)

1cm (¹⁄₂in)

5mm (¹⁄₄in)

2cm (³⁄₄in)

1 ⋆ Making the flower

* Take around 1m (1yd 4in) of tiger tail, leaving 3cm (1¹⁄₄in) at one end, and follow the diagram below to make eight stems around 2cm (³⁄₄in) long, ending in little bouquets of three to five 5mm (¹⁄₄in) sprigs. Thread a bead on to the end of each one, alternating iridescent transparent rocaille beads and iridescent white mini rocaille beads.
* Then make four 1cm (¹⁄₂in) stems in the same way.

5mm (¹⁄₄in)

2cm (³⁄₄in)

3cm (1¹⁄₄in)

2 ⋆ Arranging the pistils

Make a corolla with the large stems and place the little ones in the centre.

3 ⋆ Making the stem

* Make a final, 2cm (³⁄₄in) stem by twistin the thread with the 3cm (1¹⁄₄in) sprig set aside at the start. End with a little loop which you attach the earring fastening. Cut off the excess thread.
* Create a second, identical earring.

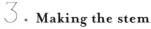
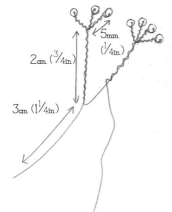
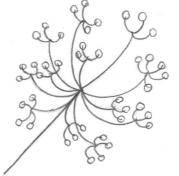

...Thread, fabric and ribbons...
* white sewing thread
* 2 x 5cm (2in) of white lace ribbon 1.5cm (⅝in) wide
* 4 pink pistils available from haberdashers'
* white fabric and light green satin

...Accessories and tools
* needle
* scissors
* pair of earring fastenings

Delicate bells

1 * Making the little bell

· Sew a gathering thread along the long edge of one of the pieces of ribbon (see page 6). Gather the ribbon right up and tie the thread ends together to make the shape of a bell. Sew the ribbon very finely to close it up.

2 * Adding the pistils

· Turn the little bell inside out to hide the stitching inside. Thread a sewing needle and pass it through the centre. Fold in half two strands of pink pistils; hang these over the thread and return the needle back through the lace. Pull the thread tight so that the pistils are hanging from the centre.

3 * Finishing the earring

· Cut out a flower 2cm (¾in) in diameter from the white fabric and two leaves 1cm (½in) and 1.5cm (⅝in) in length from green satin. Thread the flower on to the little bell knot the thread 5mm (¼in) above, then thread on the smallest leaf. Knot the thread again and attach the large leaf. If the satin frays, stabilize it with some textile hardener or paste.
· Attach the earring fitting with a simple knot
· Make a second identical earring.

Actual size

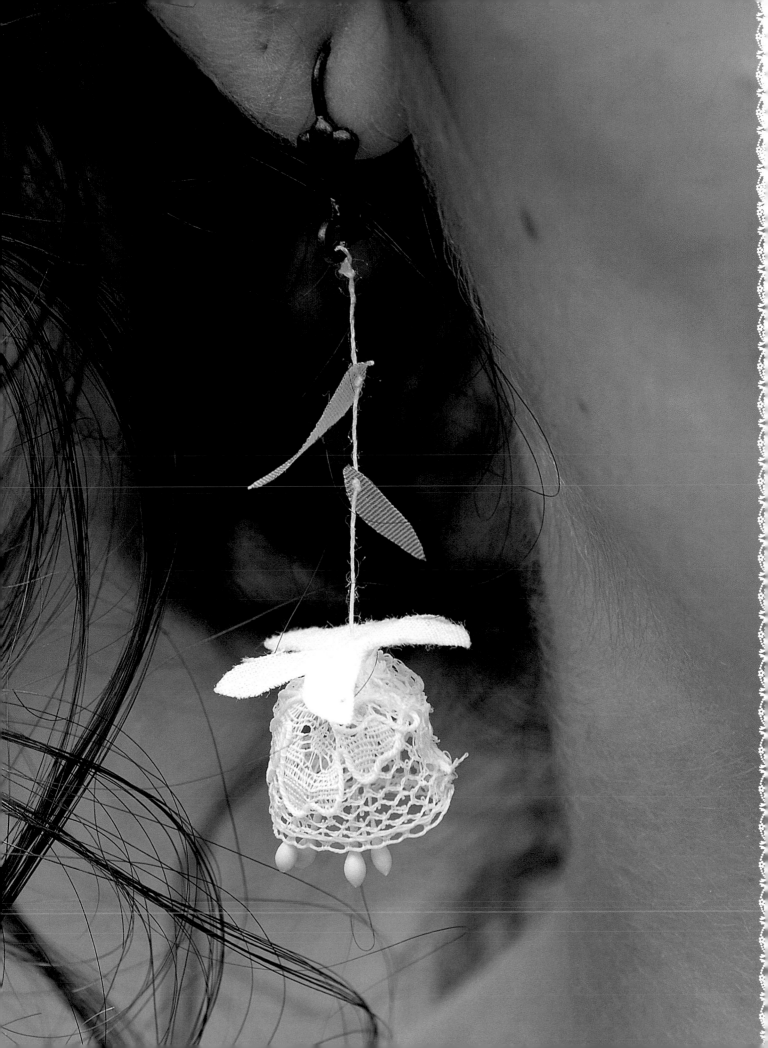

...Thread and fabrics...
* organza, white cotton and white tulle
* beige sewing thread

...For the beautiful flower...
* 15 transparent gold rocaille beads
* 5 small light pink crystals

...Accessories and tools for each ring
* scissors
* band ring
* needle

4cm (1½in)

3cm (1¼in)

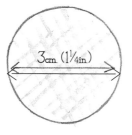

3cm (1¼in)

Fairy fingers

A fabric flower

1. Preparing the flower

· Cut out a 4cm (1½in) flower from the organza, another 3cm (1¼in) one from the white cotton and a circle 3cm (1¼in) in diameter from the white tulle. Overlay the three pieces and sew the beads and crystals into the centre of the flower to secure the layers.

2. Making up the ring

· Stitch the flower pieces to the ring. This is a light and radiant ring to wear.

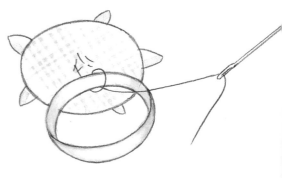

* beige sewing thread
* 10cm (4in) ribbon in beige tulle,
  3cm (1¼in) wide
* 80cm (31in) very fine tiger tail

...For the beaded flower...
* 120 small transparent rocaille tube beads
* 3 opaque gold rocaille beads
* 3 transparent gold rocaille beads

A beaded flower
for a fairy finger

3 * Adding the pistils and ellipse

· In the centre, create six twisted pistils
about 1.5cm (⅝in) long. Thread a gold
rocaille bead on to the end of each one.
Then make some little loops with the tiger
tail and attach everything to the ring
(see diagram 2 on page 24).

1 * Making the bulb

· Sew the ends of the tulle ribbon together,
then run a gathering thread along each
side and pull up. You will get a sort of
ball shape. Flatten this gently.

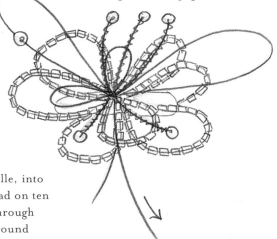

2 * Making the petals

· Stick the tiger tail through the tulle, into
the centre of the circle, and thread on ten
to twenty tube beads. Pass back through
the tulle to make a loop. Make around
seven further petals, each with ten to
twenty beads.

...Thread and beads...
- white sewing thread
- 30 transparent green rocaille beads
- 25 transparent gold rocaille beads

...Some treasures...
- 6 little beige flower sequins
- 5 little flowers in white velour

...Accessories and tools...
- 2 chignon pins
- needle
- scissors

Spring flowers

. * . * . * . * . * . * . *

Little daisies for a chignon

1 . Making the daisies

- Tie a thread around the chignon pin, then thread on some green rocaille beads; add a beige flower sequin and then another little green rocaille bead. Pass the thread back through the flower and the four beads that form the stem, pull tight and secure the thread. Make another flower in the same way.
Vary the length of the stems by threading between three and eight beads.

For the first pin, use four beige flower sequins with twenty green beads and three white velour flowers with fifteen gold beads. Keep the remaining flowers and beads for the second pin.

...Thread, ribbon and beads...
- green stretch netting
- white sewing thread
- white tulle ribbon
- 15 white rocaille beads

...Accessories and tools...
- scissors
- needle
- 2 chignon pins

The daisies

1 ★ Making up the centre of the flower

· Cut a circle with a 3cm (1¼in) diameter from the green netting and some strips that can be used as stuffing. Place the strips on to the circle and gather the edges into the centre by gradually overcasting them with tiny stitches, to form a ball.

2 ★ Making the petals

· Cut strips around 5cm (2in) long from the white tulle ribbon. Arrange them in a star shape at the base of the ball. Sew them to the centre and sew some small stitches around the edge as shown to direct the petals upwards.

3 ★ Finishing the flower

· Sew eight white rocaille beads on to the top of the ball and attach everything to the pin. To make the second, smaller flower, cut a circle with a 2cm (¾in) diameter and proceed as indicated above. Sew just seven beads on to the centre.

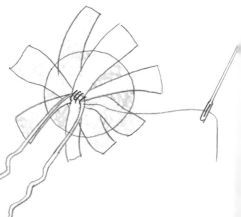

In the evening when it's quiet and peaceful why not retreat to a

secluded hideaway and write down your secrets, dreams and desires?

Create your very own notebook and pencil for your writing and a

lucky charm to bring you good fortune.

In your magical bubble you cannot be disturbed and all your

CHERISHED TREASURES are kept safe.

...Notebook, thread and fabrics...
* rectangular notebook of your choice
  (the notebook in the photo measures
  14cm x 21.5cm (5½in x 8½in))
* light blue chine felt the size of the
  notebook and 2 flaps to slip over the cover
* netting in white, green and gold
* sewing thread in off-white and
  aniseed green
* mohair wool in light green

...For the little flowers...
* 9 white sequins
* 12 gold sequins

* 25 large transparent
  tube beads (5mm (¼in))
* 28 translucent blue rocaille beads
* 16 translucent green rocaille beads
* 35 gold rocaille beads
* 10 iridescent white round beads
* 23 small transparent
  tube beads (2mm (⅛in))
* 13 iridescent green sequins
* 1 sequin in the shape of a little
  white flower
* 18 silver mini-sequins

...Foliage...
* artificial bay leaf in green, mounted
  on wire
* little corolla in serrated metal
* ivy leaf in khaki green velour

...Accessories and tools
* scissors
* pins
* needle
* crochet hook (size 4)

Secret notebook

1. Preparing the cover

· Measure the notebook, allowing a 5mm
(¼in) margin on all sides, and cut out the
felt required.

· Adjust the pattern to the size of your
notebook and cut out the flowers in the
different colours of netting. Pin them on
to the felt, following the suggested pattern
as closely as possible.

· Take 1.5m (1yd 23in) of sewing thread
(use more later if needed) and fold in half
to make it thicker, then start sewing stems
using backstitch (see page 6). Attach the
flowers, sewing around the edges using the
same stitch. Add some small stitches in the
aniseed green thread.

2. Sewing on the beads and sequins

· Sew six sequins in a circle in the centre
of the large white flower on the left.
Partially cover them with a second,
smaller circle.

· In the centre, make the pistils with
sixteen large transparent tube beads.
Make five large ones by placing two
tubes end to end and six little ones
with just one tube. Use six translucent
blue rocaille beads and five
translucent green ones to block the
tubes by passing the thread back
through them as in the diagram.

· In the same way, distribute the beads and
sequins over the other flowers by
following the diagram (see page 34).

Secret notebook, page 32 (enlarged to 120 per cent)

Star pencil, page 37 (actual size)

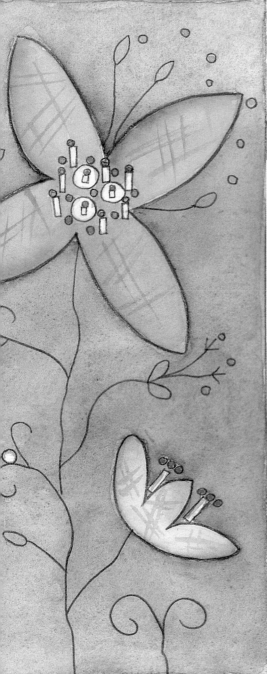

5 * Stitching around the edge

· Fold 1.5m (1yd 23in) of sewing thread in half and sew around the edge of the cover with blanket stitch (see page 6), joining the two pieces and including the flaps in the sewing.

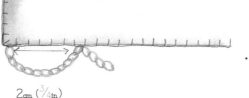

2cm (¾in)

3 & 4 * Making up the cover

· Cut two strips 5cm (2in) wide and the same height as the notebook (not forgetting the margins) from the light blue felt. They will serve as flaps to slip the cover into.

· Pin the pieces together carefully – the cover and the strips – so that you can easily sew them.

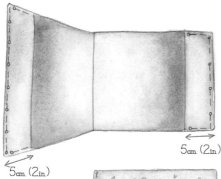

5cm (2in)

5cm (2in)

6 * Making the lacy edging

· Catch the end of the mohair wool in the fold of the cover, using the blanket stitch edging to attach it. With the crochet hook, make a chain stitch of about ten links that you attach to the border every 2cm (¾in), by simply passing the wool through one of the blanket stitches. Continue in this way right around the edge of the cover.

7 * Making the closure

· Finish by attaching the clasp. Make a small hole in the centre of the right side of the notebook; and insert the wire with the bay leaf, topped with the little metal corolla. Twist the wire into a spiral at the back of the felt.

· Then stick the stem of the ivy leaf on to the opposite side, between the two thicknesses of felt, and twist the end in the same way so that it stays in place.

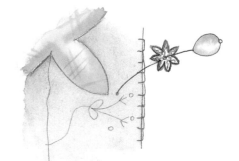

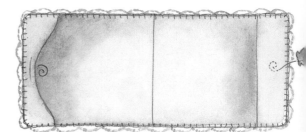

* pencil
* around 15cm (6in) of tubular netting in green (to fit the size of the pencil)
* nylon sewing thread
* strip of beige tulle (3cm x 30cm (1¼in x 12in))
* netting in iridescent green and white

... white acrylic paint

...Some beads and sequins...
* 12 gold sequins
* 13 iridescent white round beads
* 6 x 5mm (¼in) transparent tube beads
* 6 x 2mm (⅛in) transparent tube beads
* 12 translucent blue rocaille beads

...Accessories and tools
* paintbrush
* glue gun
* needle
* scissors

Star pencil

2 * Preparing the star

· Sew a gathering stitch using the nylon thread along the length of the strip of tulle, 3mm (⅛in) from the edge. Then join the ends of the thread and make a double knot pulled tightly. Drop a blob of glue on to the top of the pencil and apply the tulle star.

1 * Covering the pencil

· Paint the pencil white and leave to dry. Slide the tubular netting over it and attach it at the top using the glue gun.

3 * Finishing the bouquet

· Cut a large flower from the green netting and a small flower from the white netting. Stick them to the centre of the tulle star.

· Sew six sequins in a circle in the middle of the white flower; make another smaller circle in the same way, using six sequins. Stick the iridescent white round beads in the centre, overlapping one another. Finally, using the nylon thread, sew the stamens of the flower all around the sequins: they are formed from tube beads, each topped with a blue rocaille bead. Alternate large and small tubes.

...Ring, thread and fabrics...
* tiger tail in gold
* key-ring around 2.5cm (1in) in diameter
* 20cm (8in) of gold ribbon, 3mm (⅛in) wide
* patterned fabric in beige tones
* sewing thread in beige
* embroidery thread in gold and sparkling white

...Foliage...
* 1 ivy leaf in green velour
* small green artificial bay leaf, mounted on wire
* 1 sequin in the shape of a white flower

...Some treasures...
* 3 small feathers
* selection of 8 x 10cm (4in) pieces of ribbon, yarn, tulle, organza, wool and lace in shades of green, white and gold

* 2 small gold bells
* 1 mirror disc 1.5cm (⅝in) in diameter
* 1 green crystal
* 1 gold rocaille bead

...Accessories and tools
* glue gun
* scissors
* needle
* small ball of cotton wool

Lucky charm

1 * Preparing the ring
· Wrap 10cm (4in) of tiger tail around the key-ring, making five little loops at equal distances apart. Then cover with gold ribbon, gluing the ends. Leave only the loops sticking out.

2 * Making a heart
· Cut two shapes from the beige patterned fabric and lay them back to back. Embroider the edge with blanket stitch (see page 6). Before closing, stuff with cotton wool.

3 * Making a plume
· Tie the three feathers together using tiger tail. Make a small attaching loop. Add a drop of glue, if needed, to strengthen the charm.

4 * Finishing the lucky charm
· Attach the various elements to each loop. Attach the ribbons with sewing thread.
– 1st loop: three types of ribbons, then 10cm (4in) of gold embroidery thread with a bell.
– 2nd loop: ivy leaf and lace.
– 3rd loop: heart and bell, attached to the end of a piece of sparkling white embroidery thread.
– 4th loop: a pretty ribbon and feathers attached to a strand of wool.

– 5th loop: two ribbons, artificial bay leaf, mirror disc and flower sequin hung from a piece of sparkling white thread. The flower sequin is topped with a green crystal and a rocaille bead.

· You can adapt the hanging items as you wish. Why not replace the artificial bay leaf with something pretty that you have found outdoors?

...Thread and fabrics...
* felt in white, red, pink and 2 shades of green
* very fine wire
* sewing thread in white, green, orange and pink
* cotton wool
* 2 small discs of white fabric, 5mm (¼in) in diameter, for the eyes
* carded wool in brown, pink and light green
* fine tiger tail

* nylon sewing thread
* netting in gold
* tulle in beige

...Beads and sequins...
* around 25 red beads and 45 green beads
* around 30 small silver sequins

...Accessories and tools
* scissors
* cutting pliers
* flat-nosed pliers
* very fine felt needle
* fine pointed tool
* pins
* needle

Little doll

Leaves scale 60 per cent.
Cut out 15 leaves

1 * Preparing the body
· Cut the shape of the body twice from white felt (see template, page 43). Take around 1.2m (1yd 11in) of wire and twist it to form the outline of a person by following the inside edge of the pattern, so that it will fit perfectly. Using the flat-nosed pliers, accentuate the angles and join the two ends of the wire together.
· Using white sewing thread, attach the wire shape to the felt by making a few stitches at strategic points (feet, hands, neck and head).

2 * Stuffing the body
· Cover with the second felt shape, then sew the layers together with blanket stitch (see page 6). Stuff with cotton wool as you go along. Use a fine pointed tool to stuff the narrow areas.

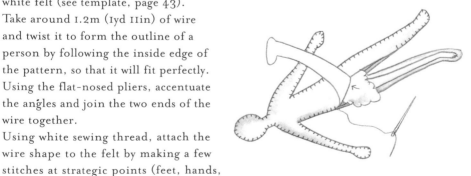

3 * Making the clothes
· Cut out the dress twice in red felt, the collar trim in pink felt, then fifteen leaves from the green felts, varying the sizes. Take two pieces of sewing thread in different colours, then embroider the veins on the leaves. Alternate white, orange and green threads.

4 ⋆ Making the dress

· Pin the dress to the body and close up the sides with blanket stitch: start at the bottom of the dress and work up, making sure to include both thicknesses of red felt in the sewing.

· For the armhole, continue stitching on a single thickness by going around the shoulder before rejoining the sewing under the arm.

· Place the collar trim on to the neckline of the dress and attach it with two stitches at the shoulders.

5 ⋆ Attaching a flounce of leaves

· Pin the leaves to the bottom of the dress at the front and back, before sewing them on with one stitch. Attach the red beads and little sequins at the top of the leaves. Sew a necklace of green beads to the edge of the collar trim. And now the little fairy is dressed!

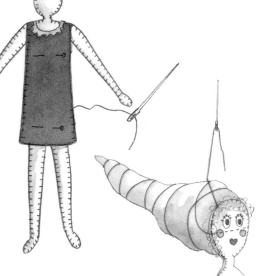

6 ⋆ Making the face

· Place the small white fabric discs where the eyes should be and sew them on with green thread, embroidering five lashes for each eye.

· For the pupil, sew a little stitch in brown carded wool. Carefully insert the needle into the wool at the point where you want to integrate it; the fibres of the wool will mix with those of the felt.

· Attach a little pink wool to the felt to make the cheeks and the mouth.

7 ⋆ Making the hair

· Place a skein of carded green wool on the fairy's head. Insert approximately 30cm (12in) tiger tail into the head via the stitching. Wrap it around the wool to make a cone. To fix the hair permanently, sew with the nylon thread around the edge of the face, catching the wool of the hair into the sewing.

8 ⋆ Attaching the wings

· Cut out the wings from the gold netting and then from the beige tulle, leaving a small margin around the edge. Pin both to the back of the doll; place the netting on top of the tulle. Attach with a stitch at the centre.

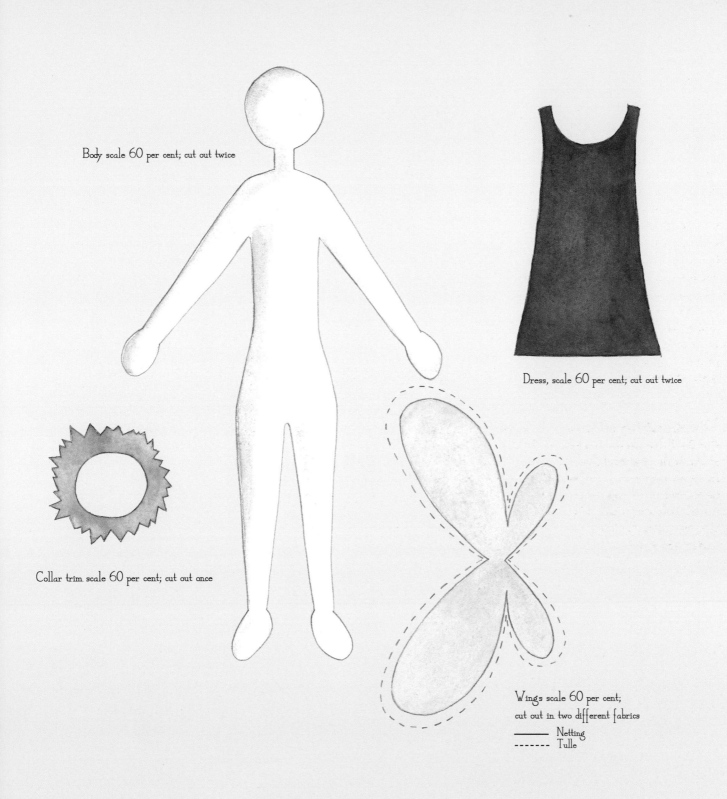

Body scale 60 per cent; cut out twice

Dress, scale 60 per cent; cut out twice

Collar trim scale 60 per cent; cut out once

Wings scale 60 per cent;
cut out in two different fabrics
———— Netting
-------- Tulle

...Fabrics...
* silk organza in pink
* sequined netting in green

...Thread and ribbons...
* sewing thread in beige
* 50cm (20in) of ribbons in green organza, green satin and rippled gold cotton

...4 small gold bells

...Accessories and tools
* scissors
* pins
* needle
* safety pin
* sewing machine (if possible)

Gossamer purse

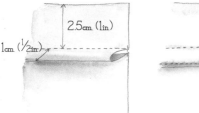

2.5cm (1in)

1cm (½in)

1 ⋆ Preparing the purse
· For the bottom, cut out a circle 17cm (6½in) in diameter from the organza, and two others from the netting. Pin the netting circles on the organza one.
· Cut out a 135cm x 24cm (53in x 9½in) strip from the organza. Create a 1cm (½in) wide hem, 2.5cm (1in) from the top edge, by folding as in the diagram above. Sew a seam along the bottom of the fold. Fold it back over the fabric, and stitch the second side to keep the hem flat over the whole strip.

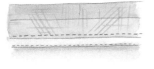

2 ⋆ Adding a gathered frill
· Cut a 135cm x 8cm (53in x 3in) strip from the green netting. Fold it in half lengthways and pin it before sewing to the upper seam of the hem.

3 ⋆ Attaching the bottom
· Gather the lower edge of the organza strip until it is 49cm (19in) in length; knot the thread. Pin the gathered edge around the overlaid circles, positioning the netting circle and the hem to the outside.
· Sew the pieces using backstitch, then turn inside out: the green circle, the hem and the netting band are inside the purse.

4 ⋆ Shutting the purse
· Finally, join the ends of the organza strip by sewing on the inside, leaving the hem open.
· Thread the three ribbons into the hem using a safety pin, then hang the little bells on the ends of the green ribbons.

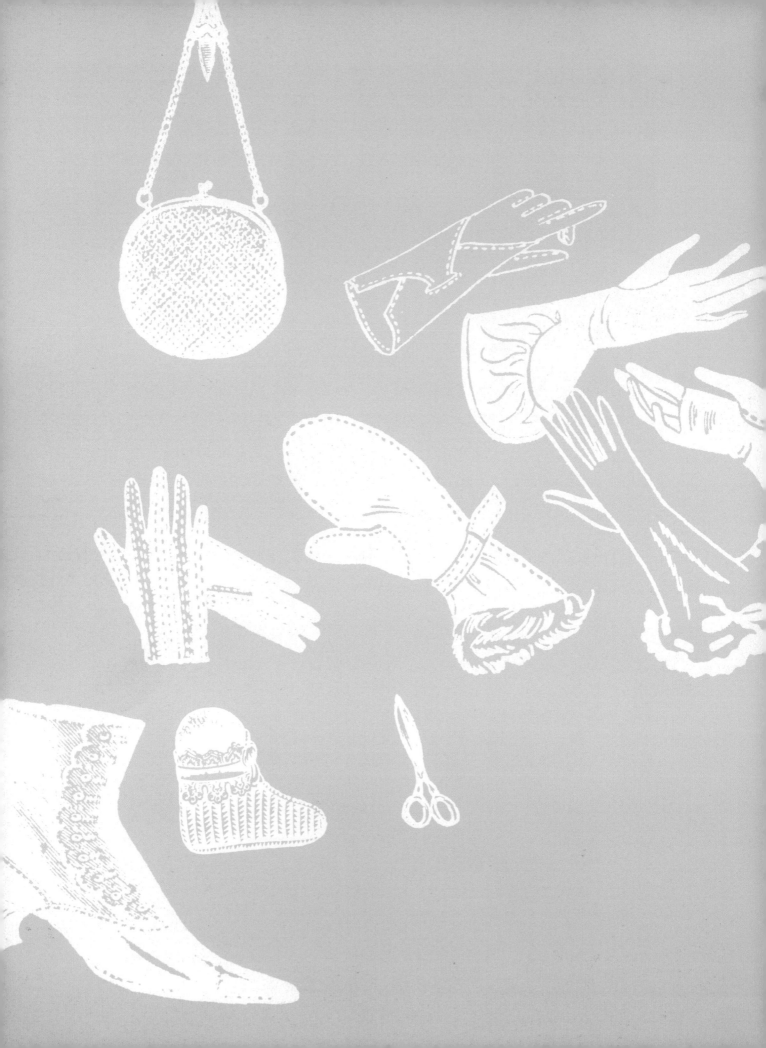

When the weather is cold the best thing to do is to stay
at home and curl up by the fire. Wrap up in your
CHIC CLOTHES and stay warm and cosy while
you watch the rain pour down outside.

...Thread and wool...
* pretty, shimmering white wool
* white wool
* white tulle for knitting
* nylon sewing thread

...For the glittering look...
* assortment of beads and crystals in shades of white, transparent, irridescent, gold and light pink

...Accessories and tools...
* pair of knitting needles (size 10)
* crochet hook (size 4 or similar)
* needle

Glittering cuffs

2 * Applying a fringe
· Turn the cuff inside out. At one of the ends, use the crochet hook to decorate each stitch with two loops of tulle measuring 1.5-2.5cm (⅝-1in) long.

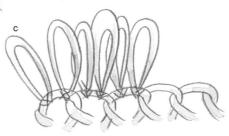

1 * Making the cuff
· Knit a square 20 x 20 stitches in stocking stitch. If you don't know this technique, cut, then hem the sleeves of an old jumper. Line up the sides of the square to make a tube and secure by inserting a strand of wool in between the stitches using a crochet hook. Do this 'sewing' on the reverse.

3 * Sewing on the beads and crystals
· Then add a row of extra loops with the pretty, shimmering wool. Take the needle and nylon thread and sew numerous beads and crystals under the rows of loops.
· Make the second cuff in the same way.

a

b

c

...Fabrics...

* 1m x 1m (1yd 4in x 1yd 4in) of linen
* 1m x 1m (1yd 4in x 1yd 4in) of green satin

...Threads and ribbons...

* sewing thread in beige
* 2m (2yd 7in) of tulle ribbon, 3cm (1¼in) wide
* nylon sewing thread
* 70cm (27½in) of organza ribbon in beige, 1cm (½in) wide

* 32cm (12½in) of satin ribbon in khaki green, 3mm (⅛in) wide
* 48cm (18¾in) pretty lacy ribbon in aniseed green
* 43cm (16¾in) pretty ribbon in sparkling light green

...Flowers and some treasures...

* 4 small gold bells
* 2 wooden buttons in the shape of a leaf
* 4 pink pistils
* 2 velour flowers in light green

* 2 corollas in serrated metal, in the shape of a flower
* 2 smaller corollas in serrated metal
* 30 gold rocaille beads
* 6 white rocaille beads

...Accessories and tools

* scissors
* pins
* needle
* iron
* sewing machine (if possible)

Elfin cape

1 * Preparing the cape

* The cape is made up of two identical pieces for the front and a single piece for the back. The pattern allows for seams 1cm (½in) from the edge. Cut out the pieces from the linen first, then from the satin, as follows:
  – for the front: cut out the shape of the cape twice in each fabric;
  – for the back: pin the template (see page 53) on to the linen folded in half. Line up the straight edge of the pattern with the fold line in the fabric; then cut around the edges of the template. Remove and unfold the fabric. Repeat with the satin;
  – for the hood: cut out the shape twice in each fabric and place to one side.

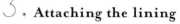

Diagram of the opened-out cape

2 * Assembling the pieces

* For each fabric (outer and lining), place the back piece on to the side pieces, right sides facing, and sew together with running stitch.

3 * Attaching the lining

* Then place the linen and satin pieces right sides together. Pin the sides and scalloped bottom before sewing them. Snip the edges, don't close up the neck.

4 * Making the hood

* Assemble the two pieces for the hood in each fabric.

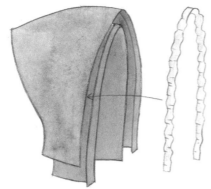

5 ⋆ Attaching the frill

· Gather the edge of a tulle ribbon 1.6m (1yd 27in) long to obtain a length of 70cm (27½in) (see page 6).

· Using the iron, mark a 1cm (⅜in) fold towards the reverse of the fabric around the edge of the hood, in the linen and in the satin. Place the two folds edge to edge and pin, slipping the gathered ribbon between the two thicknesses. Sew by hand using overcast stitch (see page 6), carefully joining the three thicknesses with the nylon thread.

6 ⋆ Snipping the edges

· Turn the hood inside out and snip the seams at the curves and points.

7 ⋆ Attaching the hood

· Turn the garment right sides out and iron the seams flat. Put together the linen parts of the hood and the cape.

· Close up the lining by pinning and sewing the bottom of the hood and the neckline of the cape with an overcast stitch. Use the nylon thread to make an invisible seam. Stitch here and there in the linen seam to keep the cape and its lining together.

8 ⋆ Attaching the ribbons and fastening

· Cut two 32cm (12½in) organza ribbons. Undo 1cm (½in) of the seam on each side of the neckline and slip in the ribbons. Close up the seams again. Hang a little gold bell on to the ends. Randomly add three pretty ribbons; conceal the point where they are attached with the buttons in the shape of a leaf.

· Make two little bells using 10cm (4in) of tulle ribbon for each one (see page 22). Hang two pistils in the centre. Then thread a green velour flower topped with a serrated metal corolla and attach everything to the end of the satin ribbon.

9 ⋆ Adding a pompom

· Carefully unpick the seam in the point of the hood, so that you can slip in some pretty ribbons and some satin ones, as well as the end of an organza ribbon 6 cm (2¼in) long. Close up again. Attach two bells to the end of the ribbons.

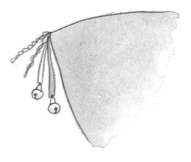

10 ⋆ Finishing touch

· Attach a thread to the end of the sparkling ribbon and thread a little metal corolla to the end. Make three pistils in gold rocaille beads, finishing with a white bead. Vary their lengths by using three, four or five gold beads.

Cut out the hood twice in the satin and twice in the linen. (scale 25 per cent)

* Cut out the front twice in the satin and twice in the linen. (scale 25 per cent)

Half of the back fold the linen fabric in half and cut out once. Fold the satin in half and cut out once. (scale 25 per cent)

...Threads and fabrics...

* 45cm x 60cm (17½in x 23½in) of white felt, 5mm (¼in) thick
* sturdy sewing thread in beige (buttonhole thread)
* 2 strips 8cm x 100cm (3in x 1yd 4in) of printed cotton fabric in shades of green
* nylon sewing thread
* 2 strips 6cm x 100cm (2¼in x 1yd 4in) of beige tulle

* 2 strips 2.5cm x 100cm (1in x 1yd 4in) of iridescent blue-green organza

...Some treasures...

* selection of 160 iridescent green and gold sequins
* assortment of 100 crystals in green, gold, copper and transparent
* assortment of rocaille beads in shades of green, blue, transparent and gold

* 4 fabric ivy leaves in 2 different shades

...Accessories and tools

* scissors
* pins
* needle
* iron

Pointed slippers

Approximate size EUR 39, UK 6, US 7.5

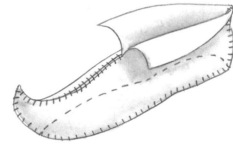

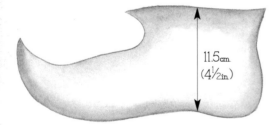

11.5cm (4½in)

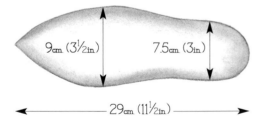

9cm (3½in)   7.5cm (3in)

← 29cm (11½in) →

1 • Preparing the slippers

* Reproduce the slipper pattern. To adjust it to your shoe size, enlarge it using the photocopier.
* Cut out the sole twice from the felt and the sides four times.
* Pin the pieces to one another. First join the sole to the sides with sturdy sewing thread using blanket stitch (see page 6); then continue with sewing the point and top seam, without sewing right to the end, then the back of the slipper.

2 • Adding the frill

* Mark a 1cm (½in) fold on the two long sides of a strip of green cotton using the iron. Fold the 1m (1yd 4in) strip in half Gather each edge to obtain a 32cm (12½in) strip (see page 6). Sew the ends together inside out.

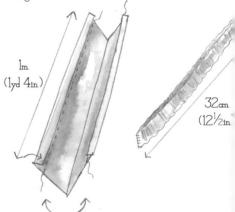

1m (1yd 4in)

32cm (12½in)

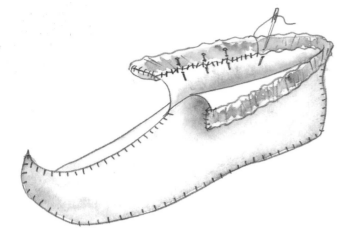

4 ★ Adding an edging

· Turn the strip right side out and hang it around the top of the slipper and even out the gathers. Pin and attach the strip by sewing the inside edge first, then the outside edge, with an overcast stitch and nylon thread. Carefully remove the gathering threads.

5 ★ Adding a tulle frill

· Gather the strip of beige tulle by sewing a gathering thread 1cm (½in) from the edge, on one side only. Gather up to obtain a length of 32cm (12½in) and knot the thread. Sew the strip on to the top of the slipper under the green cotton using nylon thread.

· Then gather the organza strip by sewing the thread along the middle this time. Fray the edges a little and sew it to the same seam as the tulle.

6 ★ Sewing on the sequins

· Prepare two selections of around forty sequins in iridescent green and gold. Sew them to the sides of the slipper using nylon thread.

· Take an assortment of around fifty crystals and some rocaille beads and sew a sprinkling of beads and crystals all around the green cotton strip; insert the thread inside the strip, then bring the needle out to thread three to seven rocaille beads in one colour, a crystal and another rocaille bead. Pass the thread back through the crystal and the beads before inserting back into the fabric. Continue by varying the colours.

· Finally, sew the stems of the two ivy leaves into the top seam of the slipper.

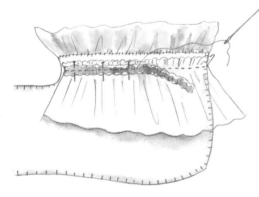

...Threads and fabrics...
- 30cm x 40cm (12in x 15½in) of white felt, 5mm (¼in) thick
- sturdy sewing thread in beige (buttonhole thread)
- 2 strips 7cm x 40cm (2¾cm x 15½in) of printed cotton fabric in shades of beige

- nylon sewing thread
- 2 strips 4cm x 35cm (1½in x 13½in) of beige tulle
- 2 pink organza ribbons, 1.5cm (⅝in) wide and 30cm (12in) long

...Some treasures...
- 40 gold sequins

- 24 sequins in the shape of little flowers, in shades of pink and white
- 2 little flowers in pink fabric, 3cm (1¼in) in diameter
- 2 beige flower sequins, 1.5cm (⅝in) in diameter
- 10 transparent gold rocaille beads

Child's slippers

approximate size for a 2-year-old

1 ∗ Preparing the slippers
- Refer to the instructions for the large slippers, simply adjusting the number and size of the decorations suggested.
- Gather and overlay the strips of cotton and tulle, and the organza ribbons in the same way. Fold the fabrics more to adjust their lengths to the ankle of the slipper.

2 ∗ Sewing on the sequins
- Sew a mixture of gold sequins and flower sequins in shades of pink and white on to the sides. On the top, attach all the following firmly: a fabric flower topped with a beige flower sequin and five gold rocaille beads for the centre. Do not decorate the beige cotton strip.

11.5cm (4½in)

9cm (3½in)   7.5cm (3in)

29cm (11½in)

...A tunic, thread and ribbons...
* white tunic
* elasticized, gathered white organza ribbon (allow sufficient length for the neckline and the flowers)
* white sewing thread
* printed fabric in shades of green
* offcuts of fabric (cotton, organza, netting, tulle...) in shades of white

...Flowers and some treasures...
* 8 white fabric flowers and 1 pink one, 3.5cm (1⅜in) in diameter (gathered from artificial bouquets)
* selection of rocaille beads in iridescent white, matt white and gold
* some sequins in the shape of small pink and green flowers
* butterfly in white velour

...Accessories and tools
* scissors
* needle
* pins

Flowery tunic

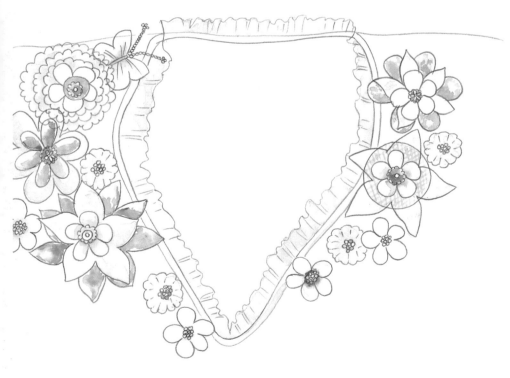

The decoration on the tunic is made from a selection of artificial flowers, as well as flowers and circles cut from different pieces of fabric. The pieces are overlaid and attached by sewing on sequins and rocaille beads. Use the pattern as an outline, then let your imagination do the rest!

1 * Applying the flowers

Cut the elasticized organza ribbon to the size of the neckline of the tunic and sew on around the neckline. Cut out flowers in various shapes from the fabrics suggested, then arrange them prettily on the tunic, along with the artificial flowers and pin. When you are happy with the design, attach them by sewing rocaille beads and sequins into the centre.

Create a poetic world brimming
with charm and light by sprinkling
your home and garden with
DAINTY DECORATIONS.

...A magic flower...
* 3 garlands of fabric leaves around 1m (1yd 4in) each
* selection of around 50 fabric flowers in various sizes and colours

...Some treasures...
* 15 large sequins in iridescent green
* 18 small gold bells
* 10 feather butterflies in several colours and 1 or 2 dragonflies

...Threads and ribbons...
* green wire, 3mm (⅛in) in diameter
* nylon thread, gold cable and flax string
* green organza ribbon
* fine wire, 1mm (¹⁄₁₆in) in diameter

... skein of light green carded wool

...Accessories and tools
* cutting pliers
* glue gun
* scissors

... 5 small glass jars and 5 tea-lights

Hanging mobile

1 ⋆ Preparing the crown
· Make a circle 60cm (23½in) in diameter by making three circles with the 3mm (⅛in) wire. Tie with the flax string at several points to keep it in place. Cover the wire by wrapping the garlands of leaves around it. Fix the ends using the glue gun. Stick around thirty fabric flowers on to the metal circle, in between the leaves.

2 ⋆ Hanging the little pots
· Tie four ribbons to four opposite points on the circle; gather up the ends and tie in a pretty bow.
· Hang the mobile at the right height to be able to continue working. Attach the five glass pots using a wire secured round the rim, spacing them 37cm (14½in) apart, so that the mobile is well-balanced.

· Decorate the top of the pots by sticking tufts of green carded wool and four little flowers around the edge. Place the tea-lights inside.
· Between each pot, and taking care to keep them a certain distance away, attach four nylon threads measuring 20-50cm (8-20in), finished with three sequins and a little bell. Drop little blobs of glue along the length of the threads.

3 ⋆ Finishing touch
· Glue seven strands of gold cable wire about 15cm (6in) long to the circle, finished with one or two little bells that you hold in place with a drop of glue.
· Then add seven strands of fine wire measuring 20-30cm (8-12in). Bend them upwards, then stick the butterflies and dragonflies to their ends. Attach the final insects to the circle, in between the leaves and flowers.

...Thread and paper...

* gold wire, 1mm (1/16in) in diameter
* tissue paper in white, light pink, light green and dark pink
* 2 strips of fine card 2.5cm x 28.5cm (1in x 11in) and 2cm x 22cm (3/4in x 8 3/4in)

...Flowers and some treasures...

* assortment of sequins in green, white and gold
* some rocaille beads in pink and gold
* 2 flowers in white fabrics
* selection of light and dark pink pistils
* around ten sequins shaped like flowers in shades of white and pink
* 3 leaves in white velour

...Accessories and tools...

* cutting pliers
* flat-nosed pliers
* glue gun
* wallpaper paste and a bowl

Pumpkin flowers

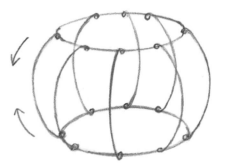

Press to bend the stems.

1 * Making the bulb

· Make two circles 10cm (4in) in diameter with two lengths of gold wire (about 35cm (13 1/2in) long). Close them by wrapping the ends around each other.
· Then cut eight 20cm (8in) stems from the wire, and distribute them around one of the circles, spacing them approximately 4cm (1 1/2in) apart. Bend the ends into a little 3mm (1/8in) hook that you attach around the circle, closing up using the pliers.
· Proceed in the same way to attach them to the second circle. Then bend the stems to make a bulb shape. If necessary, strengthen the bulb with blobs of glue.

2 * Making the cover

· Using 70cm (27 1/2in) of wire, create a circle 9cm (3 1/2in) in diameter; make it into a spiral to form a cone. Finish with a little loop at the top.
· Attach a 1.4m (1yd 19in) wire at the base and shape eight pointed 8cm (3in) petals around it. Twist a little loop at each point. Pass the wire back inside the circle between each petal and fold back using the flat-nosed pliers.

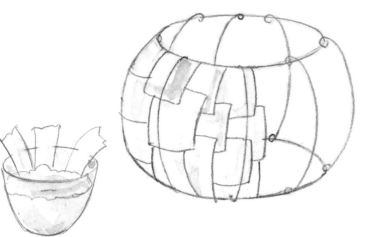

5 * Decorating the cover

· Fold the tabs towards the inside of the circle and stick them under the cover. This strip will serve to keep the cover on the bulb.

· Then decorate the hat: stick on sequins topped with little beads, and a fabric flower with pistils in the centre, and atta_ two velour leaves to the loop on the top.

3 * Making the ball

· Prepare the wallpaper paste by mixing a tablespoon of flakes in a bowl of water. Stir for a few minutes to obtain a thick paste. Tear up strips of white tissue paper, dip them in the glue, then cover the base and sides of the bulb with overlapping pieces. Leave the top circle free.

· Then apply light pink tissue paper in the same way to the petals of the cover, and green on to the cone. If the cone is too bright, tone it down by re-covering it with a layer of white paper. Leave to dry.

4 * Making a support strip

· Cut tabs 1cm (½in) wide and about 3cm (1¼in) long in the larger strip of fine card. Stick the ends of the strip together to make a circle 9cm (3½in) in diameter.

3cm (1¼in)

1mm (¹⁄₁₆in)

2.5cm (1in)

For the little flower

· Proceed as for the large flower, but by dividing the measurements by 1.4. Alter the colour of the hat by using the dark pink tissue paper, and lighter pistils on the little fabric flower. Attach a single velour leaf to the loop at the top.

...Threads and beads...
* reel of gold wire, 1mm (1/16in) in diameter
* transparent beads and pendants
* very fine nylon thread

...Accessories and tools
* flat-nosed pliers
* cutting pliers
* scissors

Sparkling pendants

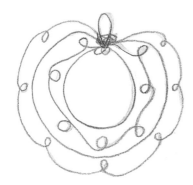

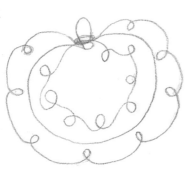

1 * Making the structure

· Start by creating a small ring at the end of the wire using flat-nosed pliers. Then bend the wire to make circles, some plain, some looped. Continue with increasingly larger circles unwinding the wire as you go. Wrap the wire around the first ring between each circle so that it is kept firmly in place. When you have finished, cut the wire with the cutting pliers.

· Vary the size of the suspensions from 10-18cm (4-7in) in diameter.

2 * Final touch

· From each circle, randomly hang beads and pendants using the nylon thread. To make them hang nicely, pass the wire back through the first beads before tying it around the circle.

· Finally, attach a nylon thread to the first ring, so that you can hang your creation wherever you wish.

...Fibres and cage
* 9 supple wicker stems approximately 65cm (25½in)
* raffia in green
* skein of carded wool in light green

...Flowers
* assortment of around 30 fabric leaves, in different shapes and colours

* approximately 15 fabric flowers, in shades of green, white, pink and violet
* 5 pompom grasses
* 3 small toadstools in red and white
* 2 little, artificial berries in red and green

...Some treasures
* butterfly in green velours
* 3 red hearts in metal, for hanging, in

3 different sizes - 4.5cm (1¾in), 2.5c (1in) and 1.5cm (⅝in) (or cut out of ca and hand-painted by you)
* little red bell

...Accessories and tools
* glue gun
* nylon thread
* scissors

Caged beauty

6cm (2¼in)

1 * Making the cage
· Bend a wicker stem into a circle with a 15cm (6in) diameter. Close it by binding the ends with some raffia.
· Place eight other wicker stems perpendicularly around the edge, with the points upwards. Space them about 6cm (2¼in) apart. To attach them, use raffia and the glue gun.

2 * Closing the cage
· Join the points with one another to form a flat star. Secure and strengthen with raffia and some blobs of glue. Leave to dry.
· To keep the wicker stems bent and so that the cage has a pretty shape, pass a nylon thread through the spot where the points join and then attach to two opposite points on the base of the circle.
· Leave the thread in place for several days to give the wicker time to dry out.

3 * Making the base
· Cross several lengths of raffia across the circle of the base. Place the skein of carded wool on top to look like a carpet of moss.

4 * Decorating the cage
· Make a pretty arrangement of leaves and flowers on the top of the cage. Keep them in place with a blob of glue or by wrapping their wire stems around the wicker. Attach some strands of raffia to the middle of the leaves, letting them hang down.
· Add some vegetation to the bottom of the cage and stick the butterfly to one o the stems.
· Hang the metal hearts at varying heights using the nylon thread, not forgetting the little bell under the central heart.
· Stick the grasses, three little toadstools and some flowers into the moss.

* old, yellowed book
* string of electric lights
* white tissue paper

* glue gun
* wallpaper paste

Garland of flowers

1 * Creating the flowers

· Tear out little strips 5-7cm (2-2¾in) long from the pages of an old book. Try to get a pointed end to the strip so that it looks like a petal. Using a glue gun, arrange the strips around the base of a bulb in a string of electric lights to make a pretty flower; allow for around fifteen to twenty petals. Repeat for each bulb in the string.

2 * Covering the wire

· Make the wallpaper paste by mixing a tablespoon of flakes in a bowl of water. Stir for a few minutes to obtain a thick paste. Tear up pieces of tissue paper, dip them in the glue and cover the whole electric wire, including the bases of the flowers, by rolling the paper around it.

3 * Making the leaves

· Then take a piece of tissue paper lightly dipped in glue and fold it over to make a pointed leaf in a lozenge shape; attach it to the garland with glue. Repeat the process between each flower and leave the whole garland to dry for a while.

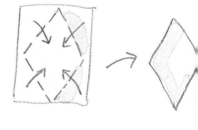

...Netting and lace...
* offcuts of white fabric in varying thicknesses and transparencies
* white tulle
* textile hardener
* 3 small offcuts of white lace, different if possible

...Accessories and tools...
* tiny pegs or paper clips
* cutting pliers
* scissors
* glue gun

... 3 small glass pots in different sizes

... Gold tiger tail

Twinkling lights

1 * Preparing the fabrics

· Coat the fabric offcuts (except for the tulle) with textile hardener. Hang them out to dry for twenty minutes. Protect the surface underneath, as the hardener can run.

2 * Making the stems

· Take a length of tiger tail the same size as the circumference of the pot that you wish to decorate. Add a margin of 5cm (2in). Lay the wire flat and fold 5cm (2in) in at one of the ends.
· Cut three wires approximately 12cm (4¾in) each and twist them at their centre around the base wire. Do not hesitate to leave them slightly off centre to vary the length of the stems. Make a little loop at the end of each one; it will serve as a support for the flower.

5cm (2in)

3 * Making the stems

· Then hang the base wire over the top of the pot, twisting the end of the remaining 5cm (2in) with the other end. Bend the stems upwards, spacing them evenly.

4 * Making the flowers

· When the fabrics are dry and hard, cut out flowers in all shapes and sizes. Use the most transparent fabrics for the largest flowers, since, as the petals are overlapping, a transparent petal cannot be seen on an opaque one.
Also cut out circles of tulle 1.5-5cm (⅝-2in) in diameter.
· Prepare different types of flower creations by sometimes inserting a tulle circle. Place a blob of glue underneath and attach them to the ends of the brass wire stems or to the mouth of the jar. Finally, glue a strip of lace around the top of the pot.
· To create a magic atmosphere, just find some little white candles that fit comfortably into the glass pots.

...Threads and fabrics...
* various fabrics in shades of green and white (satin, organza, cotton...)
* white sewing thread
* very fine silver wire

...Accessories and tools...
* scissors
* needle
* flat-nosed pliers
* cutting pliers
* glue gun

My magic bouquet

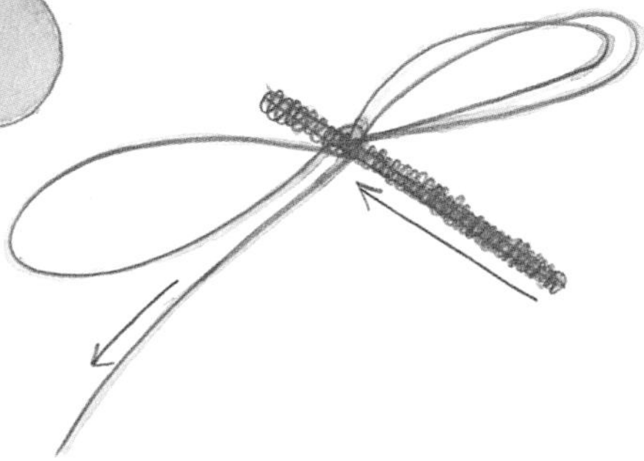

1 * Preparing the butterflies
· From the fabric, cut out three large butterflies, three little ones and six medium-sized ones. Overlay them to make three large and three medium butterflies. Sew some stitches in the centre, through all the thicknesses of fabric, to hold them together.

2 * Making the body
· Take the silver wire and start by making the body by twisting the wire around in a long loop, as in the diagram.

3 * Attaching the wings
· Next make the wings and finish with the antennae and the legs.

4 * Making the stems
· Cut some stems around 35cm (13½in) long from the wire. Bend one of their ends into a little loop. Make as many stems as the insects and butterflies. Place a blob of glue on the loops and fix the insects on top.

Then stick them into your bouquet; hollow out a cabbage or pumpkin and plant your bouquet in it.

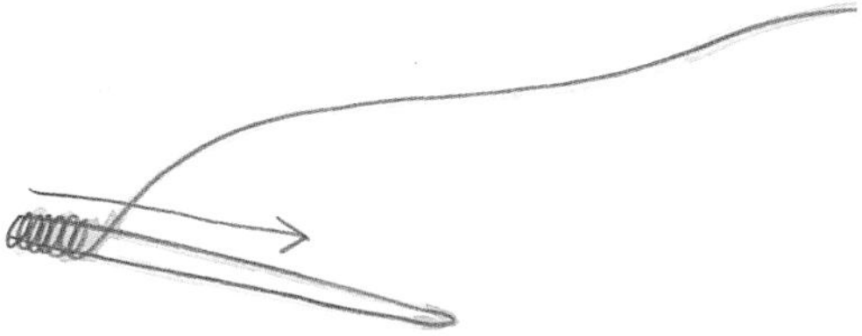

Drift away with the scent of flowers to a beautiful meadow where you will find all you need to take care of your silky soft complexion and shiny hair. In your magical world you will discover many PAMPERING BEAUTY SECRETS that you can choose to share with your friends or keep just for yourself.

...For a dazzling head of hair...
* 3 tablespoons of oat flakes,
  5 of neutral henna and
  5 of cinchona bark
* 2 egg yolks

* a tablespoon each of rum or vinegar, honey,
  castor oil, avocado oil and aloe vera gel
* some drops of essential oil - bay, lemon
  and lavender (no more than around
  ten drops in total)

Henna hair treatment

1 * Preparing the oat milk
· Soak the oats in half a glass of water for around 10 minutes, stirring from time to time. Sieve to leave just the oat milk. Put to one side.

2 * Preparing the mask
· In another bowl, mix the neutral henna and the cinchona bark; mix with a little warm water to obtain the consistency of a thick paste.

3 * Final touch
· Add all the other ingredients, ensuring that you don't exceed around ten drops of essential oils, then stir vigorously. Finally, pour the oat milk over the top and stir again. Adjust the consistency of the mask by adding some water if it is too thick or some henna if it is too runny.

4 * Applying the mask
· Apply the mask to completely cover your hair and wrap with cling film.
· Leave for at least one hour and rinse thoroughly. There is no need to use shampoo, as your hair will be clean and shiny!

...For a silky smooth complexion...

* 3 tablespoons of oat flakes and 3 of rose water
* powdered green clay
* 1 tablespoon of honey
* 1 teaspoon of rose oil
* some essential oils of your choice: tea tree, geranium, ylang-ylang (no more than around ten drops in total)
* quarter of an avocado mashed with a fork

All-natural facemask

1 * Preparing the oat milk

· Soak the oats in half a glass of water for around 10 minutes, stirring from time to time. Sieve to leave just the oat milk, then add the rose water. Scatter the powdered clay over the liquid, stirring to obtain the consistency of a thick paste.

2 * Completing the mixture

· Pour the honey, the rose oil, the essential oils (no more than around ten drops in total) and the mashed avocado into the preparation. Stir well. Adjust the consistency of the mask by adding rose water if the mixture is too thick or powdered clay if it is too runny.

3 * Applying the mask

· Chill for fifteen minutes, then apply generously to the whole of the face avoiding the eye area. Leave for at least thirty minutes, then rinse thoroughly with clean water.

· *You can keep the mask in the refrigerator for three days as long as it is covered with cling film.*

...For a twinkling hairstyle...
* tiny battery-operated string of lights
* selection of fabric flowers for the number
  of bulbs in the string of lights
* glue gun
* some clips and hairpins

Hair fireflies

· If possible, hide the battery compartment
  in the hairstyle, or leave the wire hanging
  down the back of your neck and attach the
  compartment to your clothes.

1 . Making the flower garland
· Thread the fabric flowers on to the
  little bulbs in the strip of lights and
  attach them with a blob of glue.

2 . Attaching the garland
· Scoop up your hair at the sides and the
  neck, then weave the garland into your
  hair. Hide the wire as much as possible
  with strands of hair and hold in place
  with clips and hairpins.

Invite your friends and family and cook them mouth-watering treats. For a fabulous tea party, there's nothing like TANTALIZING RECIPES. With a touch of imagination and a hint of magic, you can create a delicious feast.

...For the ice cream...
* packet of wafer biscuits
* large pot of fromage frais (soft white cheese)
* packet of frozen mixed red berry fruits

...For the coulis...
* small tub of raspberries
* small tub of strawberries
* 2 tablespoons of sugar

... and the decoration
* 6 raspberries
* 6 strawberries
* honey
* packet of tiny meringues
* some mint leaves

Ice cream with red berries

Preparation time - 20 minutes
Freezing time - 30 minutes

1 * Preparing the coulis
• Find six pretty dessert glasses. Using a knife, break up a wafer biscuit into little pieces and place in the bottom of each glass.
• Put six raspberries and six strawberries to one side for the decoration and mix the rest of the fruits with the sugar to make a coulis.
• Pour the coulis over the biscuit pieces.

2 * Preparing the cream
• Place the fromage frais and the frozen berry fruits into a mixing bowl. Gently mix together without crushing the fruits, until the fromage frais becomes a pretty pink colour. Pour 3-5 tablespoons of this preparation into the dessert glasses and stick a wafer biscuit into it.

3 * Transforming it into ice cream
• Stand the glasses in the freezer for 30 minutes until the dessert is midway between ice cream and cream. Remove just before serving. Add a strawberry, a raspberry and a teaspoon of honey to the top of each dessert. Then add a tiny meringue and a mint leaf. Finally, add a biscuit and a meringue on a cocktail stick. Now it's ready - enjoy!

If you prepare the dessert in advance, place it in the refrigerator first and only put it into the freezer 30 minutes before serving. Stick the wafer biscuits in just before freezing so that they won't turn soft.